Play Trombone Today!

A Complete Guide to the Basics

ISBN 978-1-423-42443-7

HAL•LEONARD®
CORPORATION

7777 W. BLUEMOUND RD. P.O. BOX 13819 MILWAUKEE, WI 53213

Introduction

Welcome to *Play Trombone Today!*—the series designed to prepare you for any style of trombone playing, from rock to blues to jazz to classical. Whatever your taste in music, *Play Trombone Today!* will give you the start you need.

About the CD

It's easy and fun to play trombone, and the accompanying CD will make your learning even more enjoyable, as we take you step by step through each lesson and play each song along with a full band. Much as a real lesson, the best way to learn this material is to read and practice a while first on your own, then listen to the CD. With *Play Trombone Today!*, you can learn at your own pace. If there is ever something that you don't quite understand the first time through, go back on the CD and listen again. Every musical track has been given a track number, so if you want to practice a song again, you can find it right away.

Contents

The Basics

The Parts of the Trombone

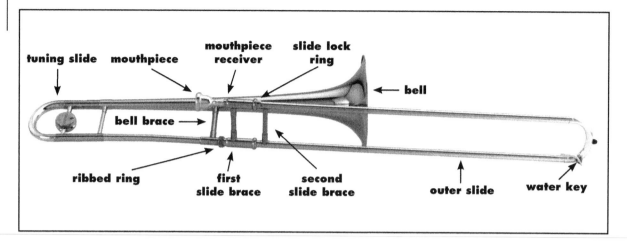

Posture

Whether sitting on the edge of your chair or standing, you should always keep your:

- Spine straight and tall.
- Shoulders back and relaxed.
- Feet flat on the floor.

Breathing & Air Stream

Breathing is a natural thing we all do constantly, but you must control your breathing while playing the trombone. To discover the correct air stream to play your trombone:

- Place the palm of your hand near your mouth.
- Inhale deeply through the corners of your mouth, keeping your shoulders steady. Your waist should expand like a balloon.
- Whisper "tah" as you gradually exhale a stream of air into your palm.

The air you feel is the air stream. It produces sound through the instrument. Your tongue is like a faucet or valve that releases or stops the air stream.

Your First Tone

Your mouth's position on the instrument is called the embouchure *(ahm' bah shure)*. Developing a good embouchure takes time and effort, so carefully follow these beginning steps:

- Moisten your lips and bring them together as if saying the letter "m."
- Relax your jaw, separating your upper and lower teeth.
- Form a slightly puckered smile to firm the corners of your mouth.
- Direct a full air stream through the center of your lips, creating a buzz. (You should buzz frequently without your mouthpiece.)
- While forming your "buzzing" embouchure, center the mouthpiece on your lips.
- Take in a full breath through the corners of your mouth and start your buzz with the syllable "tu." Your tongue will act like a valve, opening up the stream of air. Buzz through the center of your lips and try to keep the sound steady and even. This will probably feel very strange, but this buzzing is *the* fundamental sound of all brass instruments.

Reading Music

Musical sounds are indicated by symbols called **notes** written on a **staff**. Notes come in several forms, but every note indicates **pitch** and **rhythm**.

The Staff

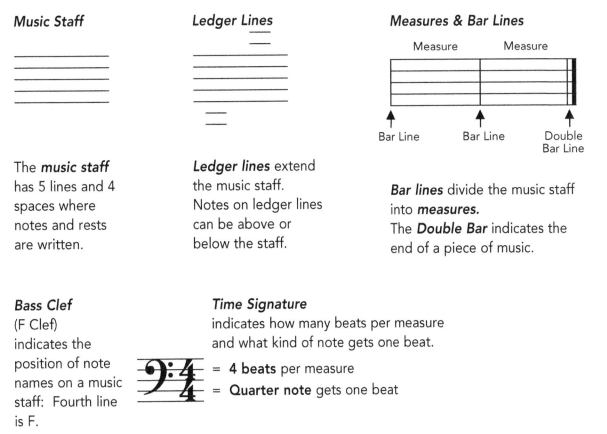

Music Staff

The **music staff** has 5 lines and 4 spaces where notes and rests are written.

Ledger Lines

Ledger lines extend the music staff. Notes on ledger lines can be above or below the staff.

Measures & Bar Lines

Measure   Measure

Bar Line   Bar Line   Double Bar Line

Bar lines divide the music staff into **measures.**
The **Double Bar** indicates the end of a piece of music.

Bass Clef

(F Clef) indicates the position of note names on a music staff: Fourth line is F.

Time Signature

indicates how many beats per measure and what kind of note gets one beat.

= **4 beats** per measure

= **Quarter note** gets one beat

Pitch

Pitch (the highness or lowness of a note) is indicated by the horizontal placement of the note on the staff. Notes higher on the staff are higher in pitch; notes lower on the staff are lower in pitch. To name the pitches, we use the first seven letters of the alphabet: A, B, C, D, E, F and G. The **bass clef** (𝄢) assigns a particular pitch name to each line and space on the staff, centered around the pitch F, located on the fourth line of the staff. Music for the trombone is usually written in the bass clef. (Some instruments may make use of other clefs, which make the lines and spaces represent different pitches.)

Note Names

Each note is on a line or space of the staff. These note names are indicated by the Bass Clef.

Sharps, Flats, and Naturals

These musical symbols are called accidentals which raise or lower the pitch of a note.

Sharp ♯ raises the note and remains in effect for the entire measure.

Flat ♭ lowers the note and remains in effect for the entire measure.

Natural ♮ cancels a flat (♭) or sharp (♯) and remains in effect for the entire measure.

Rhythm

Rhythm refers to how long, or for how many **beats** a note lasts. The beat is the pulse of music, and like your heartbeat it usually remains very steady. To help keep track of the beats in a piece of music, the staff is divided into **measures**. The **time signature** (numbers such as $\frac{4}{4}$ or $\frac{6}{8}$ at the beginning of the staff) indicates how many beats you will find in each measure. Counting the beats or tapping your foot can help to maintain a steady beat. Tap your foot down on each beat and up on each "&."

$\frac{4}{4}$ Time

Count:	1	&	2	&	3	&	4	&
Tap:	↓	↑	↓	↑	↓	↑	↓	↑

$\frac{4}{4}$ is probably the most common time signature. The **top number** tells you how many beats are in each measure; the **bottom number** tells you what kind of note receives one beat. In $\frac{4}{4}$ time there are four beats in the measure and a **quarter note** (♩ or ♪) equals one beat.

> **4** = **4 beats** per measure
> **4** = **Quarter note** gets one beat

Assembling Your Trombone

- Lock the slide by turning the slide lock ring to the right. Carefully put the slide into the bell section at a 90° angle. Tighten the connector nut to hold the two sections together.

- Carefully twist the mouthpiece into the mouthpiece receiver.

How to Hold Your Trombone

- Place your left thumb under the bell brace and your index finger on top of the mouthpiece receiver. Gently wrap your other fingers around the first slide brace.

- Place your right thumb and first two fingers on the second slide brace.

- Support the trombone with your left hand only. Unlock the slide. Your right hand and wrist should be relaxed to move the slide comfortably. Hold the trombone as shown:

Putting Away Your Instrument

Before putting your instrument back in its case, do the following:

- Blow air through the trombone while opening the water key to empty any condensation from the instrument.

- Remove the mouthpiece and slide assembly. Do not take the outer slide off the inner slide piece. Return the instrument to its case.

- Once a week, wash the mouthpiece with warm tap water. Dry thoroughly.

- Trombone slides occasionally need oiling. To oil your slide, simply:
  - Rest the tip of the slide on the floor and unlock the slide.
  - Exposing the inner slide, put a few drops of oil on the inner slide.
  - Rapidly move the slide back and forth. The oil will then lubricate the slide.

- Be sure to grease the tuning slide regularly. Your director will recommend special slide oil and grease, and will help you apply them when necessary.

Lesson 1

Track 1

The First Note: F

1

F is played in 1st position, which is where the slide is pulled all the way in. Many different notes can be played in 1st position on the trombone, so match your pitch to the CD.

Notes and Rests

Music uses symbols to indicated both the length of sound and of silence. Symbols indicating sound are called **Notes**. Symbols indicating silence are called **Rests**.

Whole Note/Whole Rest

A whole note means to play for four full beats (a complete measure in $\frac{4}{4}$ time). A whole rest means to be silent for four full beats.

Whole note	Half note	Quarter note	Eighth note
𝅝	𝅗𝅥	𝅘𝅥	𝅘𝅥𝅮
Whole rest	Half rest	Quarter rest	Eighth rest
▬	▬	𝄽	𝄾

Listen to recorded track on the CD, then play along. Try to match the sound on the recording.

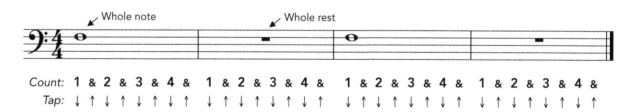

Count: 1 & 2 & 3 & 4 &   1 & 2 & 3 & 4 &   1 & 2 & 3 & 4 &   1 & 2 & 3 & 4 &

Tap: ↓ ↑ ↓ ↑ ↓ ↑ ↓ ↑   ↓ ↑ ↓ ↑ ↓ ↑ ↓ ↑   ↓ ↑ ↓ ↑ ↓ ↑ ↓ ↑   ↓ ↑ ↓ ↑ ↓ ↑ ↓ ↑

Count and Play

Notes and Rests

Quarter Note/Quarter Rest

A quarter note means to play for one full beat. A quarter rest means to be silent for one full beat. There are four quarter notes or quarter rests in a $\frac{4}{4}$ measure.

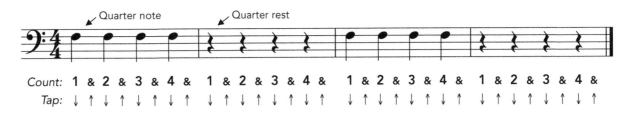

Each note should begin with a quick "tu" to help separate it from the others.

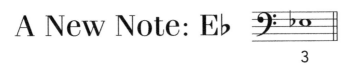

Repeat each exercise until you feel comfortable playing it by yourself and with the CD.

A New Note: E♭

Look for the position under each new note. E♭ is played in 3rd position. Practicing long tones like this will help to develop your sound and your breath control, so don't just move on to the next exercise. Repeat each one several times.

Two's A Team

Count/
Tap:

1 & 2 & 3 & 4 &   1 & 2 & 3 & 4 &   1 & 2 & 3 & 4 &   1 & 2 & 3 & 4 &

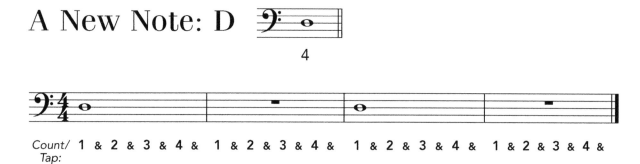

Remember: Rests are silence in music where you play nothing at all. Rests are like notes in that they have their own rhythmic values, instructing you how long (or for how many beats) to pause. Here, four beats of rest can be simplified as a whole rest.

A New Note: D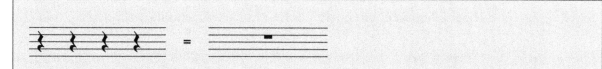

Count/
Tap:

1 & 2 & 3 & 4 &   1 & 2 & 3 & 4 &   1 & 2 & 3 & 4 &   1 & 2 & 3 & 4 &

Keeping Time

To keep a steady tempo, try tapping your foot and counting along with each song. In $\frac{4}{4}$ time, tap your foot four times in each measure and count, "1 & 2 & 3 & 4 &." Your foot should touch the floor on the number and come up on the "&." Each number and each "&" should be exactly the same duration, like the ticking of a clock.

Moving On Up

If you become winded or your lips get tired, you can still practice by positioning the notes on your instrument and singing the pitches or counting the rhythm out loud.

Count/
Tap:

1 & 2 & 3 & 4 &   1 & 2 & 3 & 4 &   1 & 2 & 3 & 4 &   1 & 2 & 3 & 4 &

A New Note: C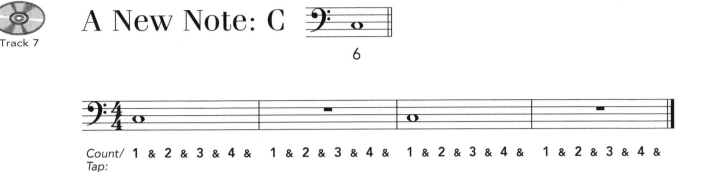

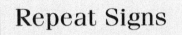

Count/
Tap: **1 & 2 & 3 & 4 &   1 & 2 & 3 & 4 &   1 & 2 & 3 & 4 &   1 & 2 & 3 & 4 &**

Four By Four

Repeat Signs

Repeat signs tell you to repeat everything between them. If only the sign on the right appears (:‖), repeat from the beginning of the piece.

Repeat sign →

Count/
Tap: **1 & 2 & 3 & 4 &   1 & 2 & 3 & 4 &   1 & 2 & 3 & 4 &   1 & 2 & 3 & 4 &**

A New Note: B♭

Count/
Tap: **1 & 2 & 3 & 4 &   1 & 2 & 3 & 4 &   1 & 2 & 3 & 4 &   1 & 2 & 3 & 4 &**

The Fab Five

1 & 2 & 3 & 4 &   1 & 2 & 3 & 4 &   1 & 2 & 3 & 4 &   1 & 2 & 3 & 4 &

First Flight

Keep the beat steady by silently counting or tapping while you play.

Rolling Along

Tonguing

To start each note, whisper the syllable "tu." Keep the air stream going continuously and just flick the tip of your tongue against the back of your upper teeth for each new note. If the notes change, be sure to move your slide quickly so that each note will come out cleanly. When you come to a rest or the end of the song, just stop blowing. Using your tongue to stop the air will cause an abrupt and unpleasant ending of the sound.

- Play long tones to warm up at the beginning of every practice session.
- Tap, count out loud and sing through each exercise with the CD before you play it.
- Play each exercise several times until you feel comfortable with it.

Track 13

Hot Cross Buns

Notes and Rests

Half Note/Half Rest

A half note means to play for two full beats. (It's equal in length to two quarter notes.) A half rest means to be silent for two beats. There are two half notes or half rests in a $\frac{4}{4}$ measure.

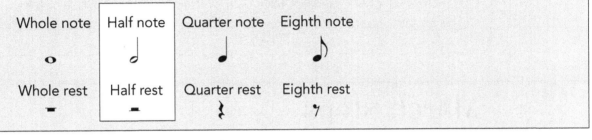

Track 14

Go Tell Aunt Rhodie

Breath Mark

The breath mark (ʼ) indicates a specific place to inhale. Play the proceeding note for the full length then take a deep, quick breath through your mouth.

Make certain that your cheeks don't puff out when you blow.

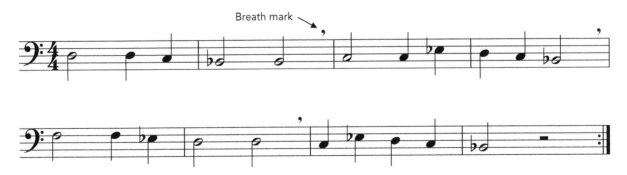

The Whole Thing

Remember: a whole rest (-) indicates a whole measure of silence. Note that the whole rest hangs down from the 4th line, whereas the half rest sits on the 3rd line.

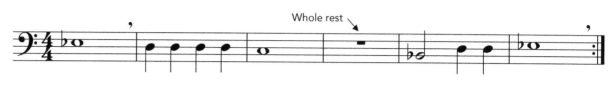

Whole rest

Key Signature – B♭

A *key signature* tells which notes are played as sharps or flats throughout the entire piece. Until now, all of the exercises have been written in the *Key of C*, which has no sharps or flats. This exercise introduces a new key signature: the *Key of B♭*. Play B♭ and E♭ throughout the piece.

March Steps

Play B♭   Play E♭

Lightly Row

14

Reaching Higher (New Note: G)

Always practice long tones on each new note.

Fermata

The fermata (⌢) indicates that a note or rest is held somewhat longer than normal.

Au Claire De La Lune

Twinkle, Twinkle Little Star

Check these points so you will get the best sound from your trombone.

- If you get a bubbling sound as you play, drain the water from the instrument by pressing the water key as you blow air (without buzzing your lips) through the trombone.

- Make certain that your cheeks don't puff out when you blow.

- Keep the center section of your lips relaxed at all times.

Deep Pockets (New Note: A)

Always practice long tones on each new note.

Doodle All Day

Try to play this on your mouthpiece only before you play it on your trombone.

Breath Support

In order to play in tune and with a full, beautiful tone, it is necessary to breathe properly and control the air as you play. Quickly take the breath in through your mouth all the way to the bottom of your lungs. Then tighten your stomach muscles and push the air quickly through the trombone, controlling the air with your lips. Practice this by forming your lips as you do when you play and then blowing against your hand. If the air is cool, you are doing it correctly. If the air is warm, tighten the lips and make the air stream smaller. Keep the air stream moving fast at all times, especially as you begin to run out of air. Practice blowing against your hand and see how long you can keep the air going. Work to keep the air stream from beginning to end.

Now try this with your trombone. Select a note that is comfortable to play and see how long you can hold it. Listen carefully to yourself to see if the tone gets louder or softer, changes pitch slightly, or if the quality of the tone changes. Do this a few times every time you practice, trying to hold the note a little longer each time and maintain a good sound.

Jingle Bells

Dynamics

Dynamics refer to how loud or soft the music is. Traditionally, many musical terms (including dynamic markings) are called by their Italian names:

f forte *(four' tay)*   loud

mf mezzo forte *(met' zoh four' tay)*   moderately loud

p piano *(pee ahn' oh)*   soft

Producing a louder sound requires more air, but you should use full breath support at all dynamic levels.

My Dreydl

Pick-up Notes

Sometimes there are notes that come before the first full measure. They are called *pick-up notes*. Often, when a song begins with a pick-up measure, the note's value (in beats) is subtracted from the last measure. To play this song with a one beat pick-up, you count "1, 2, 3" and start playing on beat 4.

Track 25

Eighth Note Jam

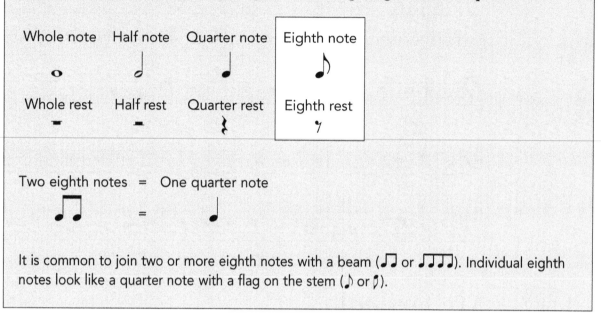

Notes and Rests

Eighth Note/Eighth Rest

An eighth note half the value of a quarter note, that is, half a beat. A eighth rest means to be silent for half a beat. There are eight eighth notes or eight eighth rests in a $\frac{4}{4}$ measure.

Whole note	Half note	Quarter note	Eighth note
o	𝅗𝅥	𝅘𝅥	𝅘𝅥𝅮

Whole rest	Half rest	Quarter rest	Eighth rest
𝄻	𝄼	𝄽	𝄾

Two eighth notes = One quarter note

𝅘𝅥𝅮𝅘𝅥𝅮 = 𝅘𝅥

It is common to join two or more eighth notes with a beam (♫ or ♫♫). Individual eighth notes look like a quarter note with a flag on the stem (♪ or ♪).

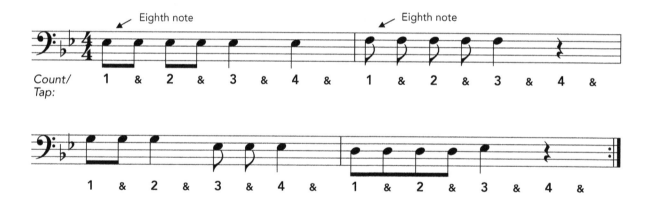

Count/Tap: 1 & 2 & 3 & 4 &   1 & 2 & 3 & 4 &

1 & 2 & 3 & 4 &   1 & 2 & 3 & 4 &

Eighth Note Counting

The first eighth note comes on "1" as your foot taps the floor. The second happens as your foot moves up on "&." The third is on "2" and the fourth is on the next "&" and so forth. Remember to count and tap in a steady and even manner, like the ticking of a clock.

Skip To My Lou

Check your hand position when holding your trombone.

Oh, Susanna

Notice the pick-up notes.

William Tell

Good posture will improve your sound.

- Support the trombone with your left hand, leaving your right hand free to move.
- Be sure to blow enough air through your trombone for a smooth, even sound. Be careful not to blow too hard or to "blast" your tone.

Track 29

Two By Two

²⁄₄ Time

A time signature of ²⁄₄ means that a quarter note gets one beat, but there are only two beats in a measure.

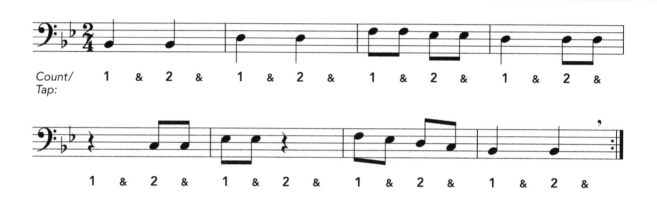

Count/
Tap: 1 & 2 &   1 & 2 &   1 & 2 &   1 & 2 &

1 & 2 &   1 & 2 &   1 & 2 &   1 & 2 &

Track 30

High School Cadets March

Tempo Markings

The speed or pace of music is called **tempo**. Tempo markings are usually written above the staff. Many of these terms come from the Italian language.

Allegro   (ah lay' grow)   Fast tempo

Moderato (mah der ah' tow)   Medium or moderate tempo

Andante   (ahn dahn' tay)   Slower "walking" tempo

Hey, Ho! Nobody's Home

Play The Dynamics

Dynamics

Gradual changes in volume are indicated by these symbols:

Remember to keep the air stream moving fast both as you get louder by gradually using more air on the crescendo, *and* as you get softer by gradually using less air on the decrescendo. Keep your embouchure firm as the dynamics change.

Frère Jacques

Hard Rock Blues

Posture

Good body posture will allow you to take in a full, deep breath and control the air better as you play. Sit or stand with your spine straight and tall. Your shoulders should be back and relaxed. Think about your posture as you begin playing and check it several times while playing.

Alouette

Tie

A **tie** is a curved line connecting two notes of the same pitch. It indicates that instead of playing both notes, you play the first note and hold it for the total time value of both notes.

 = 2 beats

Dot

A **dot** adds half the value of the note to which it is attached. A dotted half note (♩.) has a total time value of three beats:

Therefore, a dotted half note has exactly the same value as a half note tied to a quarter note.

Playing track 35 again, compare this music to the previous example:

| Dotted half note (three beats) | = | Half note (two beats) | + | Quarter note (one beat) |

Camptown Races

Always use a full air stream.

The Nobles

Notice the tie across the bar line between the first and second measure. The F on the third beat is held through the following beats 4 and 1.

Three Beat Jam

¾ Time

The next song is in ¾ time signature. That is, three beats (quarter notes) per measure.

Three beats per measure

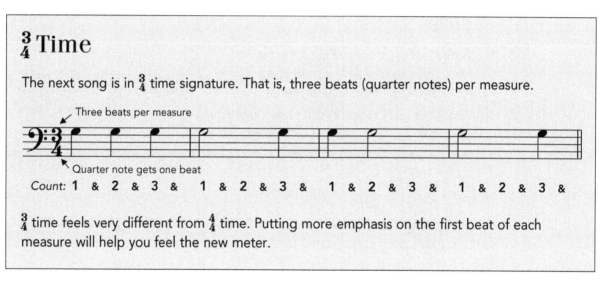

Quarter note gets one beat

Count: **1** & **2** & **3** & **1** & **2** & **3** & **1** & **2** & **3** & **1** & **2** & **3** &

¾ time feels very different from ⁴⁄₄ time. Putting more emphasis on the first beat of each measure will help you feel the new meter.

Morning (from Peer Gynt)

Hand Position

Now is a good time to go back to page 7 and review proper hand position. This is very important to proper technique. Holding the instrument properly will allow you to move your slide freely. If you feel discomfort in your left hand or arm, relax the grip of your left hand a little.

Posture also plays a role in comfort. Sitting up straight and tall and bringing the instrument **to** your embouchure allows the instrument to balance correctly, avoiding excess tension in your hands and arms.

- As you position the notes on your trombone, you can practice quietly by speaking the names of the notes, counting out the rhythms, singing or whistling the pitches, or buzzing on the mouthpiece.

- Don't let your cheeks puff out when you play.

- Keep the center section of your lips relaxed at all times.

- Use plenty of air and keep it moving *through* the instrument.

Track 40

Mexican Clapping Song ("Chiapanecas")

Accent

The accent (>) means you should emphasize the note to which it is attached. Do this by using a more explosive "t" on the "tu" with which you produce the note.

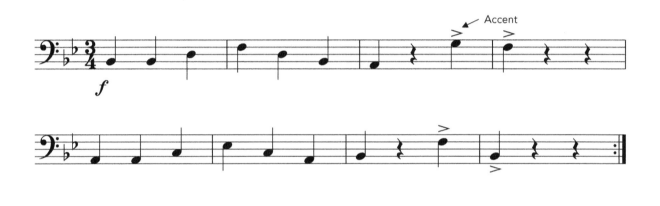

Track 41

Hot Muffins (New Note: A♭)

3

Sharps, Flats, and Naturals

Any sharp (♯), flat (♭), or natural (♮) sign that appears in the music but is not in the key signature is called an *accidental*. The accidental in the next example is an A♭ and it effects all of the As for the rest of the measure.

A **sharp** (♯) raises the pitch of a note by one half step.

A **flat** (♭) lowers the pitch of a note by one half step.

A **natural** (♮) cancels a previous sharp or flat, returning a note to its original pitch.

When a song requires a note to be a half step higher or lower, you'll see a sharp (♯), flat (♭), or natural (♮) sign in front of it. This tells you to raise or lower the note *for that measure only*. We'll see more of these "accidentals" as we continue learning more notes on the trombone.

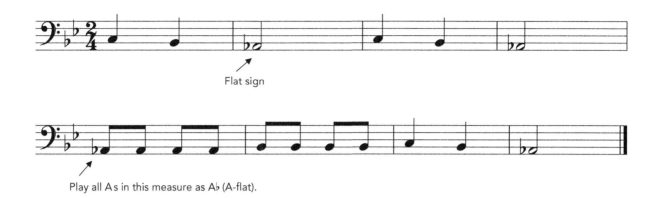

Flat sign

Play all A s in this measure as A♭ (A-flat).

Track 42

Cossack Dance

Notice the repeat sign at the end of the fourth measure. Although this particular repeat sign does not occur at the end of the exercise, it behaves just like any other repeat sign. Play the repeated section twice, then continue.

Track 43

Basic Blues (New Note: A♭)

For higher notes, don't press the mouthpiece hard against your lips. Instead, follow these suggestions:

- Firm the corners of your mouth.
- Raise the back of your tongue slightly, as if whispering "tee."
- Blow the air slightly faster through your instrument.

High Flying

Key Signature – E♭

This exercise introduces a new key signature: the **Key of E♭**. Play B♭, E♭, and A♭ throughout the piece.

1st and 2nd Endings

The use of **1st and 2nd endings** is a variant on the basic repeat sign. You play through the music to the repeat sign and repeat as always, but the second time through the music, skip the measure or measures under the "first ending" and go directly to the "second ending."

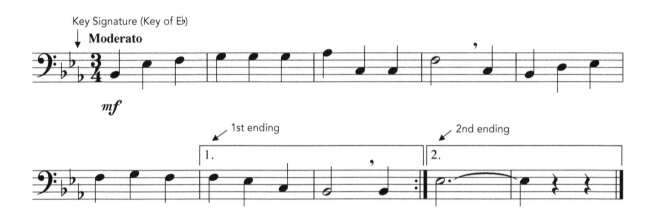

Up On A Housetop

Track 46

The Big Airstream (New Note: B♭)

Track 47

Waltz Theme

Moderato

mf *f* *mf* *f*

Track 48

Down By The Station

Allegro

mf

Track 49

Banana Boat Song

D.C. al Fine

At the **D.C. al Fine**, play again from the beginning, stopping at **Fine**. D.C. is the abbreviation for Da Capo *(dah cah' poh)*, which means "to the beginning." Fine *(fee' neh)* means "the end."

Always check the key signature.

Track 50

Razor's Edge (New Note: E)

Natural Sign

A **natural** sign (♮) cancels a flat or a sharp for the remainder of the measure.

Natural sign

p

Track 51

The Music Box

Moderato

p

Track 52

Smooth Operator

Slur

A curved line connecting notes of different pitch is called a *slur*. Notice the difference between a slur and a tie, which connects notes of the **same** pitch. Tongue the first note normally. Then, play the slurred note(s) using "dah," a legato tonguing syllable. Try to keep slurred notes as smooth and connected as possible. Keep the airstream moving through each slur. *Legato* – An Italian word for smooth and connected.

Slur

Gliding Along

This exercise is almost identical to the previous one. Notice how the different slurs change the tonguing.

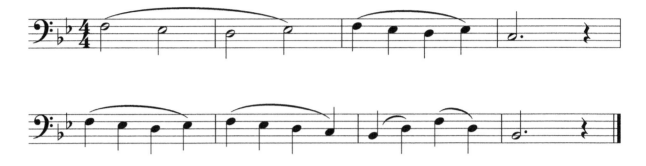

Take The Lead (New Note: A)

Trombone Rag

Glissando

The glissando is a special trombone technique used in ragtime and other styles of music. It looks like this: *gliss.*

To play a glissando, move your slide without tonguing and use a full airstream. Remember that glissandos are different from legato tonguing (slurs).

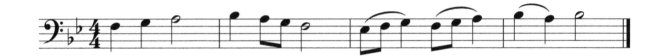

Allegro

Track 56

The Cold Wind

Phrase

A phrase is a musical "sentence," often 2 or 4 measures long. Try to play a phrase in one breath.

Track 57

Satin Latin

Key Signature – F

A key signature with one flat indicates that all written Bs should be played as B♭s.
This is the **Key of F**.

Multiple Measure Rest

Sometimes you won't play for several measures. The number above the **multiple measure rest** (𝄐) indicates how many full measures to rest. Count through the silent measures.

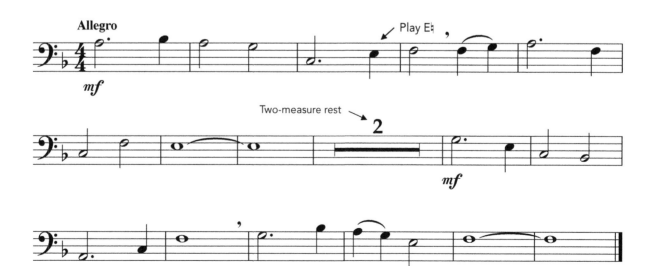

Track 58

Naturally

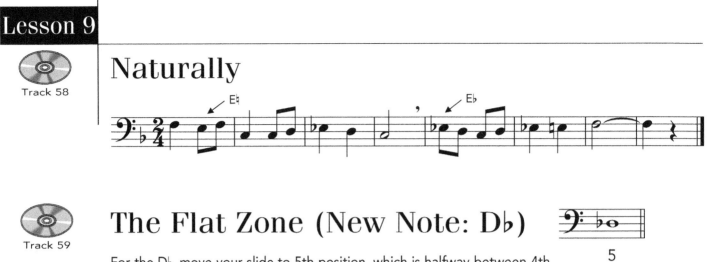

Track 59

The Flat Zone (New Note: D♭)

For the D♭, move your slide to 5th position, which is halfway between 4th and 6th. Listen carefully to match pitch of the D♭.

Track 60

On Top Of Old Smokey

Track 61

All Through The Night

Dotted Quarter Note

Remember that a dot adds half the value of the note. A dotted quarter note followed by a eighth note (♩. ♪) and (♩ ♪♪) have the same rhythmic value.

Sea Chanty

Always use a full air stream.

Scarborough Fair

Auld Lang Syne

Lesson 10

Notes that are slurred without changing the position are called **lip slurs**. Brass players practice lip slurs to develop a stronger air stream and embouchure, and to increase range. You should practice lip slurs every day. To play lip slurs well:

- Keep your throat as open and relaxed as possible. If your throat is tense, imagine that you are yawning as you play.
- While playing the first note of a lip slur, *think* the pitch of the slurred note *before* you play it.
- Keep the air stream full and steady to the end of the slur. This doesn't mean that you should play loudly, but that you should support the tone with your breath.

Track 65

Slur Exercise No. 1 (Lip Slur)

Track 66

Slur Exercise No. 2 (Lip Slur)

Track 67

Slur Exercise No. 3 (Lip Slur)

Technique Trax

Stepping Stones (New Note: C)

3

Austrian Waltz

Moderato

_f_

Michael Row The Boat Ashore

Repeat the section of music enclosed by the repeat signs (‖: ▦ :‖). If 1st and 2nd endings are used, they are played as usual—but go back only to the first repeat sign, not to the beginning.

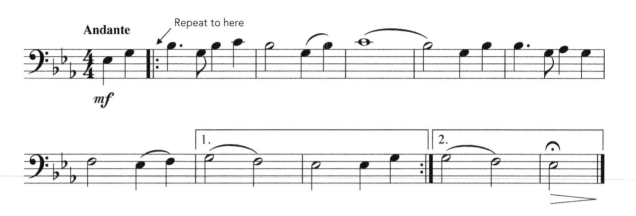

Finlandia

C Time Signature

Common time (C) is the same as $\frac{4}{4}$.

When The Saints Go Marching In

Botany Bay

The Streets of Laredo

Trombone Scales and Arpeggios

Key of B♭

1.

2.

3.

4.

Trombone Scales and Arpeggios

Key of E♭

1.

2.

3.

4.

Trombone Scales and Arpeggios

Key of F

1.

2.

3.

4.

Trombone Scales and Arpeggios

Key of A♭   Play all As as A-flat and all Ds as D-flat.

Position Chart for Trombone

E

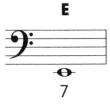

7

F

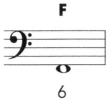

6

F♯ G♭

5

G

4

G♯ A♭

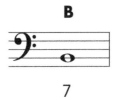

3

A

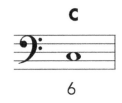

2

A♯ B♭

1

B

7

C

6

C♯ D♭

5

D

4

D♯ E♭

3

E

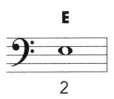

2

F

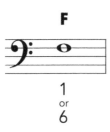

1
or
6

F♯ G♭

5

A♯ B♭

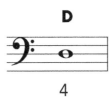

B

Position Chart for Trombone

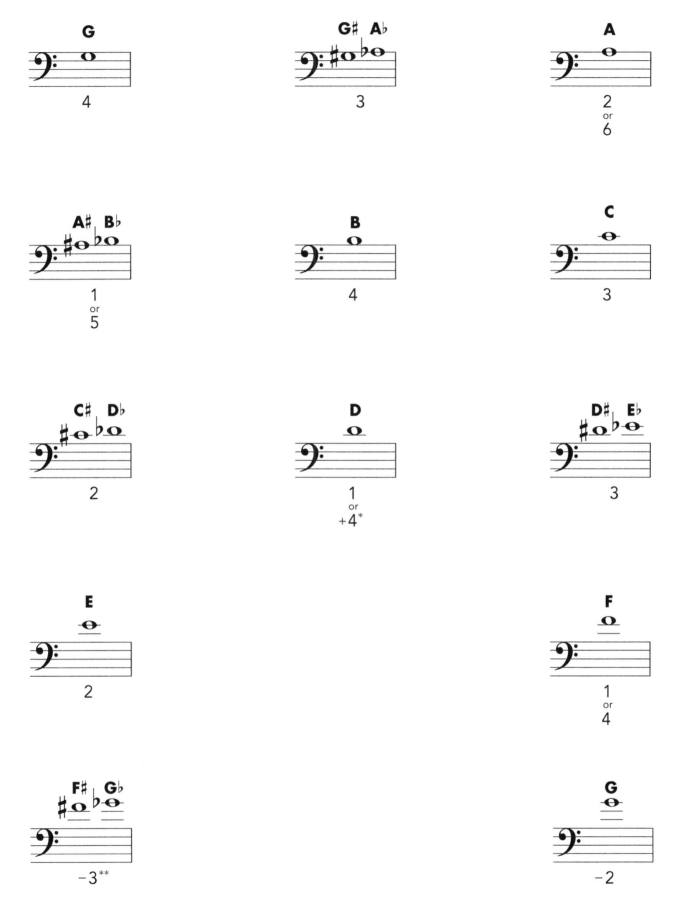

* + = Make the slide a little longer.
** − = Make the slide a little shorter.

Glossary of Musical Terms

Accent	An Accent mark (>) means you should emphasize the note to which it is attached.
Accidental	Any sharp (♯), flat (♭), or natural (♮) sign that appears in the music but is not in the key signature is called an Accidental.
Allegro	Fast tempo.
Andante	Slower "walking" tempo.
Arpeggio	An Arpeggio is a "broken" chord whose notes are played individually.
Bass Clef (𝄢)	(F Clef) indicates the position of note names on a music staff: The fourth line in Bass Clef is F.
Bar Lines	Bar Lines divide the music staff into measures.
Beat	The Beat is the pulse of music, and like a heartbeat it should remain very steady. Counting aloud and foot-tapping help maintain a steady beat.
Breath Mark	The Breath Mark (ʼ) indicates a specific place to inhale. Play the proceeding note for the full length then take a deep, quick breath through your mouth.
Chord	When two or more notes are played together, they form a Chord or harmony.
Chromatic Notes	Chromatic Notes are altered with sharps, flats and natural signs which are not in the key signature.
Chromatic Scale	The smallest distance between two notes is a half-step, and a scale made up of consecutive half-steps is called a Chromatic Scale.
Common Time	Common Time (𝐂) is the same as $\frac{4}{4}$ time signature.
Crescendo	Play gradually louder. (*cresc.*)
D.C. al Fine	D.C. al Fine means to play again from the beginning, stopping at Fine. D.C. is the abbreviation for Da Capo, or "to the beginning," and Fine means "the end."
Decrescendo	Play gradually softer. (*decresc.*)
Diminuendo	Same as decrescendo. (*dim.*)
Dotted Half Note	A note three beats long in duration (𝅗𝅥.). A dot adds half the value of the note.
Dotted Quarter Note	A note one and a half beats long in duration (♩.). A dot adds half the value of the note.
Double Bar (𝄁)	Indicates the end of a piece of music.
Duet	A composition with two different parts played together.

Dynamics	Dynamics indicate how loud or soft to play a passage of music. Remember to use full breath support to control your tone at all dynamic levels.
Eighth Note	An Eighth Note (♪) receives half the value of a quarter note, that is, half a beat. Two or more eighth notes are usually joined together with a beam, like this: ♫
Eighth Rest	Indicates 1/2 beat of silence. (♪)
Embouchure	Your mouth's position on the mouthpiece of the instrument.
Enharmonics	Two notes that are written differently, but sound the same (and played with the same fingering) are called Enharmonics.
Fermata	The Fermata (⌒) indicates that a note (or rest) is held somewhat longer than normal.
1st & 2nd Endings	The use of 1st and 2nd Endings is a variant on the basic repeat sign. You play through the music to the repeat sign and repeat as always, but the second time through the music, skip the measure or measures under the "first ending" and go directly to the "second ending."
Flat (♭)	Lowers the note a half step and remains in effect for the entire measure.
Forte (𝑓)	Play loudly.
Half Note	A Half Note (♩) receives two beats. It's equal in length to two quarter notes.
Half Rest	The Half Rest (▬) marks two beats of silence.
Harmony	Two or more notes played together. Each combination forms a chord.
Interval	The distance between two pitches is an Interval.
Key Signature	A Key Signature (the group of sharps or flats before the time signature) tells which notes are played as sharps or flats throughout the entire piece.
Largo	Play very slow.
Ledger Lines	Ledger Lines extend the music staff. Notes on ledger lines can be above or below the staff.
Mezzo Forte (𝑚𝑓)	Play moderately loud.
Mezzo Piano (𝑚𝑝)	Play moderately soft.
Moderato	Medium or moderate tempo.
Multiple Measure Rest	The number above the staff tells you how many full measures to rest. Count each measure of rest in sequence. (▬▬)
Music Staff	The Music Staff has 5 lines and 4 spaces where notes and rests are written.

Glossary continued

Natural Sign (♮)   Cancels a flat (♭) or sharp (♯) and remains in effect for the entire measure.

Notes   Notes tell us how high or low to play by their placement on a line or space of the music staff, and how long to play by their shape.

Phrase   A Phrase is a musical "sentence," often 2 or 4 measures long.

Piano (p)   Play soft.

Pitch   The highness or lowness of a note which is indicated by the horizontal placement of the note on the music staff.

Pick-Up Notes   One or more notes that come before the first full measure. The beats of Pick-Up Notes are subtracted from the last measure.

Quarter Note   A Quarter Note (♩) receives one beat. There are 4 quarter notes in a $\frac{4}{4}$ measure.

Quarter Rest   The Quarter Rest (𝄽) marks one beat of silence.

Repeat Sign   The Repeat Sign (:‖) means to play once again from the beginning without pause. Repeat the section of music enclosed by the repeat signs (‖: ≡ :‖). If 1st and 2nd endings are used, they are played as usual—but go back only to the first repeat sign, not to the beginning.

Rests   Rests tell us to count silent beats.

Rhythm   Rhythm refers to how long, or for how many beats a note lasts.

Scale   A Scale is a sequence of notes in ascending or descending order. Like a musical "ladder," each step is the next consecutive note in the key signature.

Sharp (♯)   Raises the note a half step and remains in effect for the entire measure.

Slur   A curved line connecting notes of different pitch is called a Slur.

Tempo   Tempo is the speed of music.

Tempo Markings   Tempo Markings are usually written above the staff, in Italian. (Allegro, Moderato, Andante)

Tie   A Tie is a curved line connecting two notes of the same pitch. It indicates that instead of playing both notes, you play the first note and hold it for the total time value of both notes.

Time Signature   Indicates how many beats per measure and what kind of note gets one beat.

Treble Clef (𝄞)   (G Clef) indicates the position of note names on a music staff: The second line in Treble Clef is G.

Trio   A Trio is a composition with three parts played together.

Whole Note   A Whole Note (𝅝) lasts for four full beats (a complete measure in $\frac{4}{4}$ time).

Whole Rest   The Whole Rest (𝄻) indicates a whole measure of silence.